GW00835918

PROGRESSIVE

Complete
Learn To Play

FINGERPICKING GUITAR
Manual

by
Brett Duncan

Visit our Website
www.learntoplaymusic.com

Contact us via email
info@learntoplaymusic.com

Like us on Facebook
www.facebook.com/LearnToPlayMusic

Follow us on Twitter
twitter.com/LTPMusic

View our YouTube Channel
www.youtube.com/learntoplaymusiccom

Published by
KOALA MUSIC PUBLICATIONS™
PROGRESSIVE COMPLETE LEARN TO PLAY
FINGERPICKING GUITAR MANUAL
ISBN: 978-1-86469-236-5
Order Code: 69236

Acknowledgments
Cover Photograph: Phil Martin
Photographs: Phil Martin

2

CONTENTS

Introduction .... Page 4
Using the Audio 4
Using a Tuner 5
Tablature 5
Tablature Symbols 6
Chord Diagrams, Scale Diagrams 7

LESSON 1 .... **Page 8**
Fingerpicking Technique 8
Playing Position 8
Hand Technique 9
Picking the Strings 10
First Position - Right Hand 11
Picking With the Thumb 12
Combining Thumb and Fingers 13

LESSON 2 .... **Page 14**
Alternating Thumb Style 14
Picking Patterns 15
Fingerpicking Pattern One 15
Alternative Chord Fingerings 16
Changing Chords 17
Fingerpicking Pattern Two 19

LESSON 3 .... **Page 20**
More Picking Patterns 20
The Pinch 20
Fingerpicking Pattern Three 20
Fingerpicking Pattern Four 20
Fingerpicking Pattern Five 22
Fingerpicking Pattern Six 22

LESSON 4 .... **Page 26**
Second Position - Right Hand 26
Patterns One and Two - Second Pos. 26
Alternative Chord Fingerings 27
Patterns Three and Four - Second Pos. 28
Optional Bass Notes 29
Patterns Five and Six - Second Pos. 30
Moving Bass Lines 31
Adding Extra Bass Notes to a Chord 32
Bass Runs 33

LESSON 5 .... **Page 34**
Accompaniment Styles 34
Pick-Up Notes 34
Man of Constant Sorrow 34
Picking Three Notes Together 35
Banks of the Ohio 35
Songs in Three Four Time 38
The Streets of Laredo 38

LESSON 6 .... **Page 40**
Arpeggio Styles 40
The *a* finger 40
Arpeggio Pattern One 40
Arpeggio Pattern Two 41
Arpeggio Patterns Three and Four 42
Amazing Grace 42
Arpeggio Patterns, Four Four Time 44
Arpeggio Patterns Five and Six 45

LESSON 7 .... **Page 46**
The Hammer-On 46
The Pull-Off 48
The Slide 49
The Bass String Hammer-On 52
Red River Valley 52

LESSON 8 .... **Page 54**
Adding Extra Notes to a Chord 54
Basic G Chord Licks 54
Basic C Chord Licks 55
Picking Four Notes Together 55
Basic D Chord Licks 56
Combining Chord Licks 57
Basic E Chord Licks 58
Basic A Chord Licks 59
F Chord Licks - Root Six
        Major Bar Chord 60
B Chord Licks - Root Five
        Major Bar Chord 61
Fingerpicking Guitar Solo -
        Boots 'n' All 62

LESSON 9 .... **Page 64**
Fingerpicking a Melody 64
*When the Saints
        Go Marching In* 64
Sloop John B 66
Enhancing an Arrangement 67
Down in the Valley 68
Amazing Grace 69
House of the Rising Sun 70
Long, Long Ago 71

LESSON 10 .... **Page 72**
Advanced Arrangements 72
Frankie and Johnny 72
Walking Bass Line 72
*Oh, Bury Me Not On the
        Lone Prairie* 74
Country Bass Line Pattern 74
Shenandoah 76
More Bass Runs 76

LESSON 11 .... **Page 78**
Extended Chord Licks 78
Banjo Picking Style 78
Will the Circle Be Unbroken 79
Banks of the Ohio 80
El Condor Pasa 82
Mama Don't Allow 84
The Last Frontier 85

LESSON 12 .... **Page 86**
Blues Fingerpicking Guitar 86
Constant Bass Line 86
A Minor Pentatonic Scale (open position) 86
A Blues Scale (open position) 86
The Triplet Rhythm 89
The Bend 90
The Release Bend 90

LESSON 13 .... **Page 92**
Constant Bass Line in the Key of E 92
E Minor Pentatonic Scale (open position) 92
E Blues Scale (open position) 92
Vibrato 92
Turnaround Licks 93

LESSON 14 .... **Page 96**
Blues Bass Line Techniques 96
Right Hand Muting 96
Doubling the Bass Line 97
Lead-In Bass Notes 97
Blues Bass Runs 98

FIRST POSITION - RIGHT HAND

The first position allocates the first finger(*i*) of the picking hand to the second string and the second finger(*m*) of the picking hand to the first string. The thumb(*p*) will play all the bass strings.

The adjacent photo highlights the first position of the right hand fingers (*i*) and (*m*). These two fingers should be in position above the strings ready to pick.

The first example in this section is a simple right hand picking exercise. All notes on the second string are played with the first finger(*i*), the first string is played with the second finger(*m*). Remember to brace the right hand thumb(*p*) on the fourth string. This will keep the right hand steady and make it easier to get a consistent, even sound to all the notes.

2

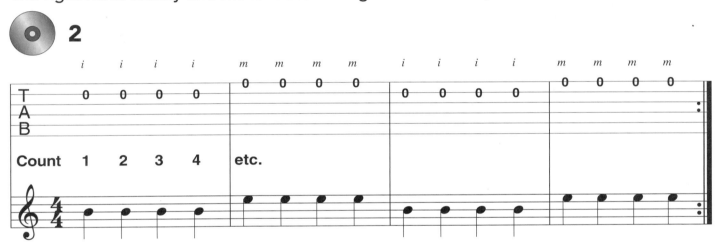

The next example is typical of the type of right hand finger movement that will feature in the early stages of this book. Try for an even, balanced movement between the two right hand fingers.

3

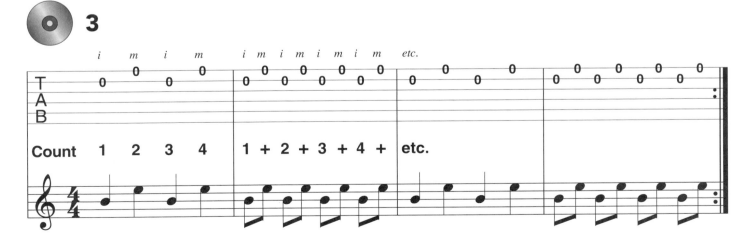

Note: It is interesting to note that in Classical guitar the above examples would most likely have been played using alternating right hand fingers.

12

PICKING WITH THE THUMB

The 4th, 5th and 6th strings are picked with the thumb (*p*). In almost all cases a free stroke is used. After striking a string the thumb should move over the third string and return to its original position ready to strike again. Your thumb should feel as if it is moving in small circles. Once again consider the two options for the position of the right hand thumb.

The classical position: The wrist is arched, thumb 45 degrees to the string and the thumbnail is used to pick the string.

The contemporary position: The wrist is kept close to the guitar face, the thumb almost parallel to the strings and the side of the thumb is used to strike the string.

Classical Position

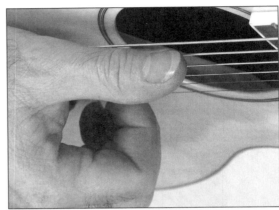

Contemporary Position

On the following recording the classical position is used on the 1st time through, the contemporary position on repeat to highlight the difference in sound when using the nail or the side of the thumb.

4

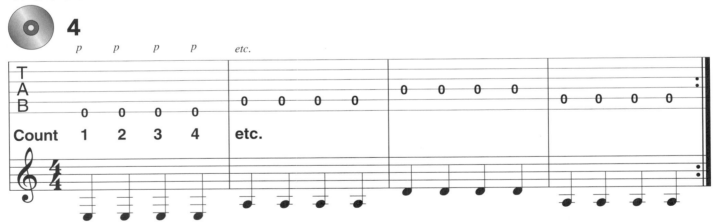

The next example is typical of the type of right hand thumb movement that will feature in the early stages of this book. This exercise requires the 2nd finger of the left hand to fret the 2nd fret of the fourth string (an E note).

5

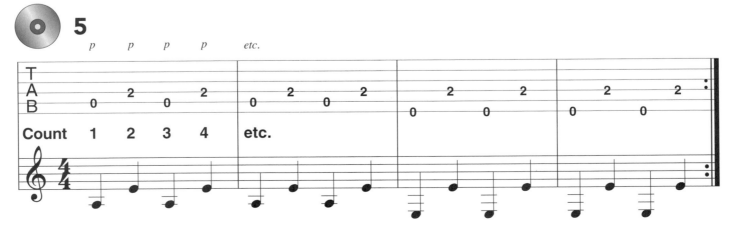

COMBINING THUMB AND FINGERS

Now it is time to try combining the picking of the strings with the right hand fingers and the right hand thumb.

The following examples features the sixth string open bass note and the bass note found on the fourth string, 2nd fret. These notes are picked with the right hand thumb(*p*). The remaining notes in each bar are the open second and first strings played with the right hand fingers (*i*) and (*m*).

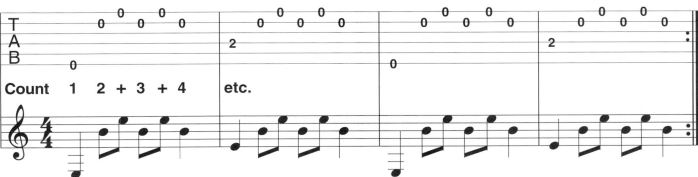

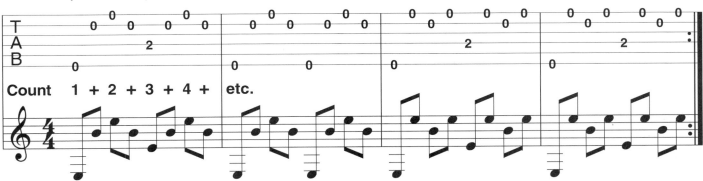

BRACING THE RIGHT HAND

Some fingerpickers prefer to use one of the following right hand bracing techniques. The first option involves resting the little finger of the right hand on the guitar face. The second option involves resting the bottom of the hand on the bridge.

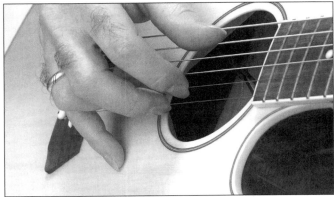

Rest little finger on guitar face.

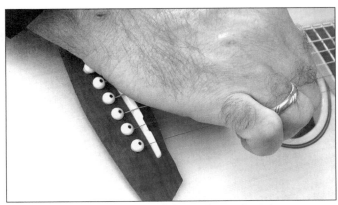

Rest bottom of hand on bridge.

FINGERPICKING PATTERN FOUR

The fourth fingerpicking pattern is the same as the previous pattern except the order of the treble strings is reversed. This time the root bass note and the first string are 'pinched' together. Compare this pattern to the third fingerpicking pattern introduced on the previous page.

optional note

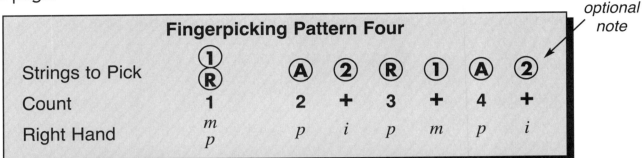

The following example uses fingerpicking pattern four.

19

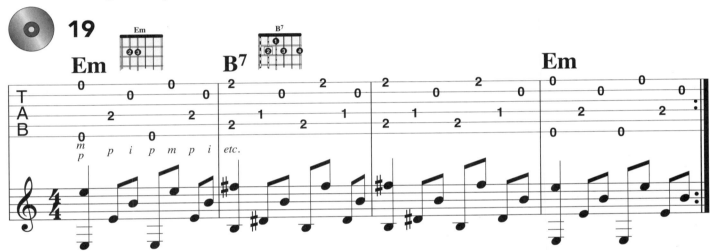

The two patterns introduced in this lesson can be used within the same progression.

20

FINGERPICKING PATTERN FIVE

The fifth fingerpicking pattern places the pinch on the second beat of the bar. This puts the emphasis or accent on this beat giving it quite a different feel to the previous patterns. The last note in this pattern is an optional note. There will be situations when you may feel more comfortable omitting this note, especially on certain chord changes and when you are changing to a different pattern which has a pinch on the first beat of the bar.

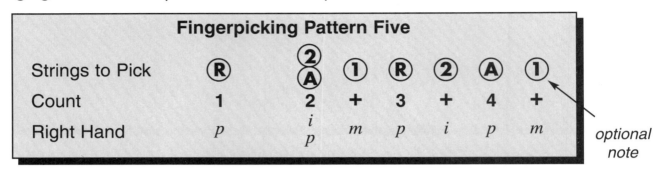

Fingerpicking Pattern Five							
Strings to Pick	Ⓡ	②Ⓐ	①	Ⓡ	②	Ⓐ	①
Count	1	2	+	3	+	4	+
Right Hand	p	i p	m	p	i	p	m

optional note

An alternative fingering for the F bar chord is introduced next. This alteration can be compared to the alternative fingering for the E chord shown on page 16. The fifth string is not picked with the right hand so it is not necessary to fret the note that is usually found on that string. Using this fingering for the F bar chord will also free up the left hand fourth finger, allowing that finger to fret other notes which can be added to the chord. This type of situation will arise later in the book.

The basic F chord used in previous exercises contained the root bass note on the fourth string. The F bar chord has a root bass note on the sixth string. This bass note is chosen as the root bass note in the following example. The fifth alternating thumb style pattern shown above is used.

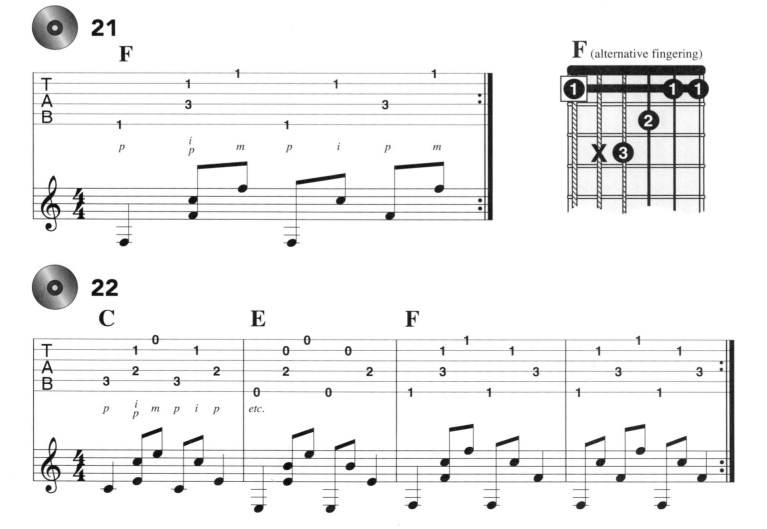

FINGERPICKING PATTERN SIX

The sixth fingerpicking pattern also places the pinch on the second beat of the bar. This pattern is the same as pattern six except the order of the first and second strings is reversed. Once again the last note in this pattern is an optional note.

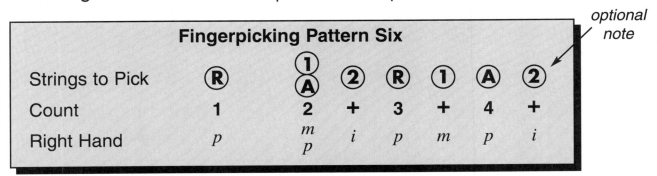

The following basic chord progression uses a combination of fingerpicking patterns five and six. You may notice the last note in the pattern has been left out in some bars. Subtle variations to the patterns can give a more natural sound to the fingerpicking.

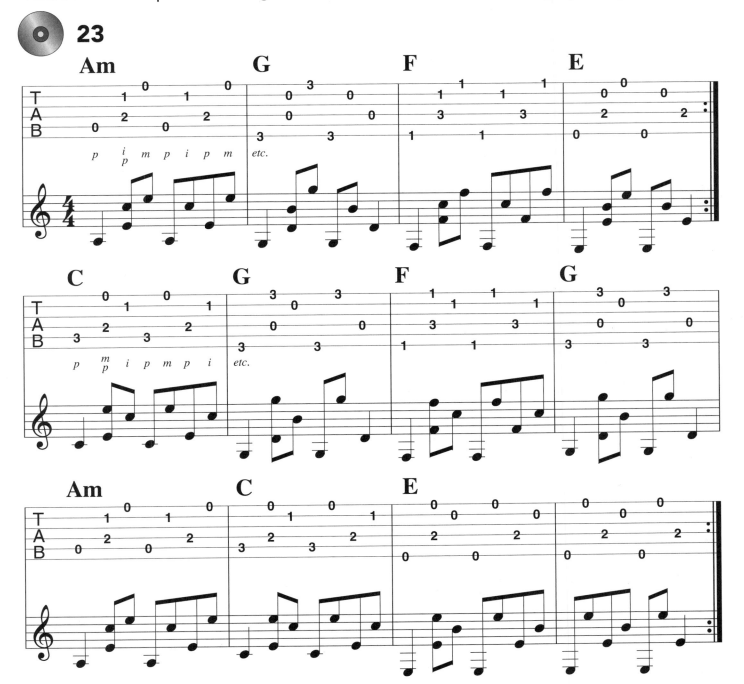

BASS RUNS

A bass run is a sequence of bass notes that ascend or descend between two chords. The common type of bass run is connecting the root bass notes of two different chords. For example, in the following exercise a bass run is used to connect the chords C to F and back again. The first bass run uses the bass notes C - D - E and F to ascend from the C chord to the F chord. These notes are then reversed to descend from the F chord to the C chord.

36

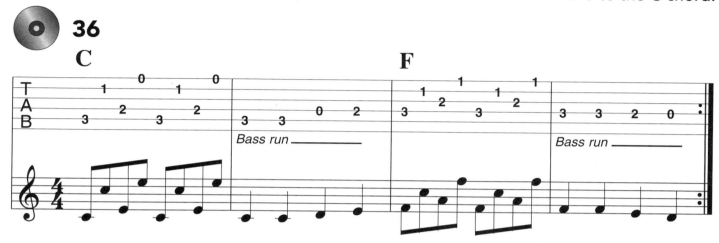

The next example uses bass runs between the G, C and D7 chords. This time the bass run is played as the picking pattern is continued with the right hand. Special attention should be given to the suggested right hand fingering.

37

Try creating you own bass runs using some of the chord progressions that have appeared in earlier examples.

LESSON FIVE

ACCOMPANIMENT STYLES

In this lesson you will learn your first basic songs and a picking pattern to accompany that song. Each accompaniment will use patterns and techniques that were studied in the previous lessons.

PICK-UP NOTES

Sometimes a song does not begin on the first beat of the bar. Any notes which come before the first full bar are called **pick-up notes**. When pick-up notes are used, the last bar is also incomplete. The combined notes in the pick-up and last bar add up to one full bar.

The following tune *Man of Constant Sorrow* begins on the second beat of the bar. The melody is relatively simple and can be played solely on the first and second strings. The chord progression to *Man of Constant Sorrow* is a sixteen bar Folk progression. Practice the melody to this song first before trying the accompaniment on the following page.

 38 Man of Constant Sorrow - Melody

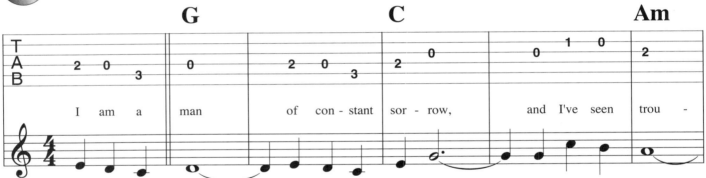

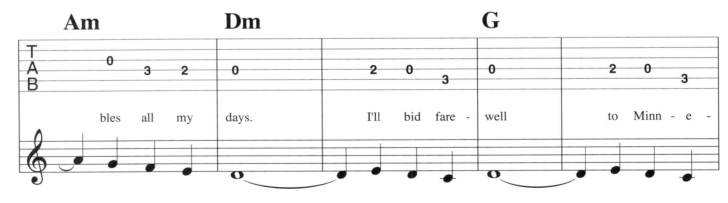

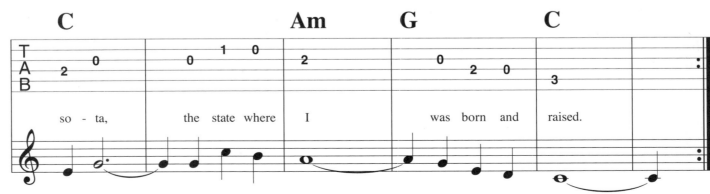

Now try the accompaniment to *Man of Constant Sorrow* which uses the first fingerpicking pattern. You may encounter difficulties with playing the pattern in time to some of the chord changes. For these instances try either omitting the last note before the chord change or substitute an open string note (see page 17).

 39 Man of Constant Sorrow

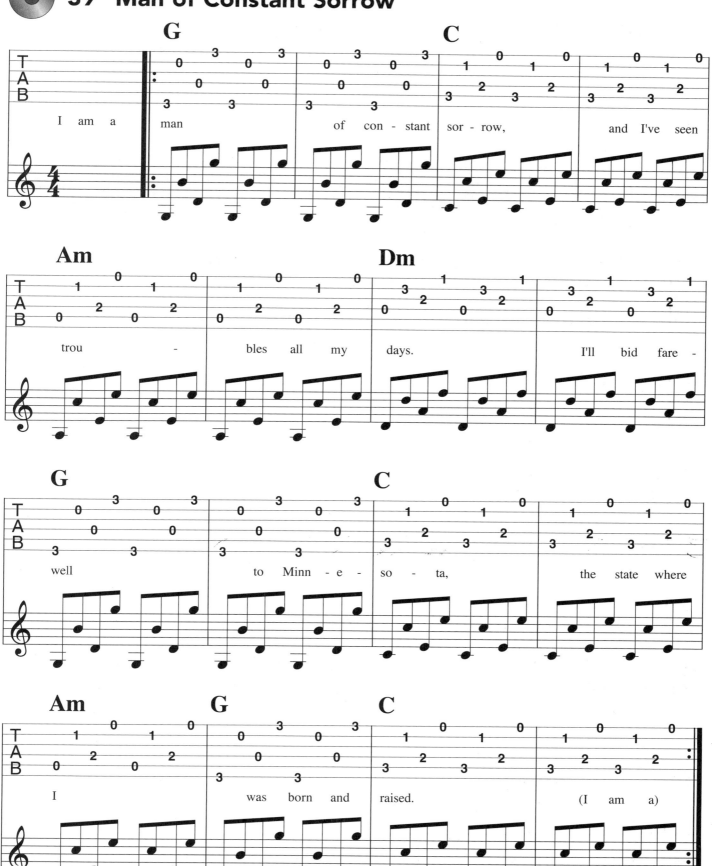

PICKING THREE NOTES TOGETHER

The picking of three notes together is when the right hand fingers pick two treble strings at the same time a bass note is picked. In the following example the *i* and *m* fingers play the first two strings at the same time. It is important to pick all strings as evenly as possible so each string has the same volume and tone.

 40

The technique described above will be employed for the accompaniment to the song *Banks of the Ohio*. First practice the melody line.

41 Banks of the Ohio - Melody

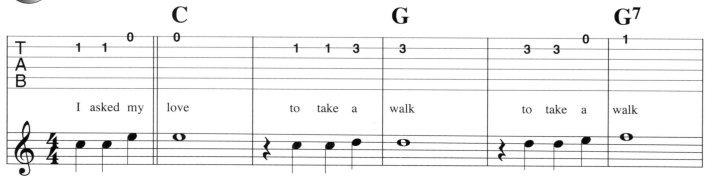

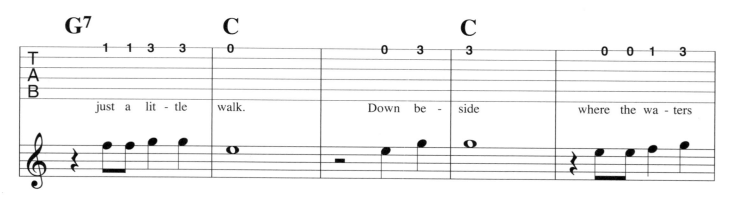

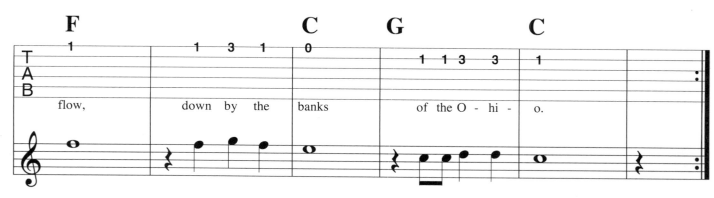

Banks of the Ohio features the chords C, F, G and G7. Several of the fingerpicking patterns studied throughout the book are used including optional bass patterns and the picking of three notes together. Bass runs are also incorporated on some chord changes.

 42 Banks of the Ohio

38

SONGS IN THREE FOUR TIME

Some songs are in three four time. Three four time is also known as waltz time. A song in three four time has the $\frac{3}{4}$ time signature at the beginning of the music notation. It indicates there are three beats (three quarter notes) in one bar of $\frac{3}{4}$ time. As there are only three beats to the bar the standard alternating bass is modified to fit into three beats.

 43

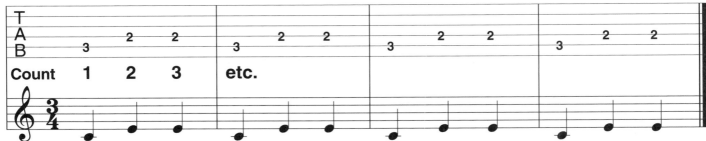

A variety of patterns can be constructed using the above $\frac{3}{4}$ bass line by incorporating notes from the treble strings.

44

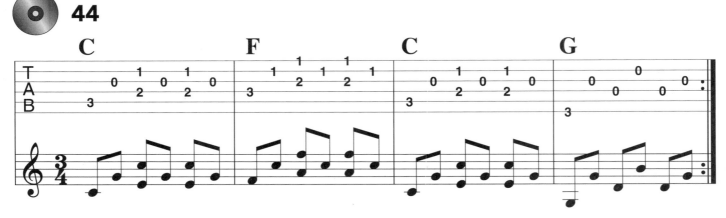

45 The Streets of Laredo - Melody

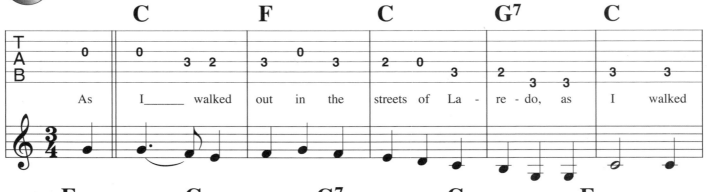

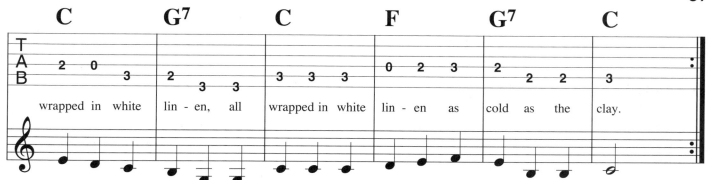

Now try the accompaniment to *The Streets of Laredo*.

46 The Streets of Laredo

LESSON SIX

ARPEGGIO STYLES

The arpeggio picking style is another common picking style used in contemporary fingerpicking guitar. This right hand style differs to the alternating thumb style in that the thumb is not putting the emphasis on every beat of the bar by playing every beat of the bar. With an arpeggio style there is no set pattern to how the right hand thumb is used. The distinguishing feature of the arpeggio style is the playing of the 'arpeggio' within a chord shape. The arpeggio refers to the notes that make up the chord. Common arpeggio playing is the playing of the notes within the chord from the lowest note to the highest note and back to the lowest note.

THE *a* FINGER

Most arpeggio patterns require the use of the right hand *a* finger. Basic arpeggio patterns allocate the right hand thumb to the root bass note, the *i* finger to the 3rd string, the *m* finger to the 2nd string and the *a* finger to the 1st string.

ARPEGGIO PICKING STYLE PATTERN ONE

The first arpeggio pattern is in $\frac{3}{4}$ time and makes use of the *i*, *m* and *a* fingers.

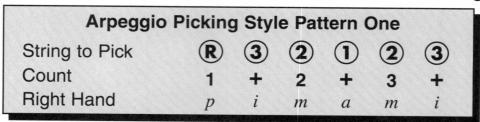

Arpeggio Picking Style Pattern One					
String to Pick	Ⓡ	③	②	①	②	③
Count	1	+	2	+	3	+
Right Hand	*p*	*i*	*m*	*a*	*m*	*i*

The above pattern is used in the following example.

🔘 **47**

ARPEGGIO PICKING STYLE PATTERN TWO

The next arpeggio pattern is also in $\frac{3}{4}$ time. This pattern is a two bar picking pattern that incorporates the alternative bass note.

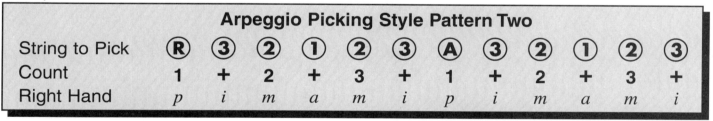

	Arpeggio Picking Style Pattern Two										
String to Pick	Ⓡ	③	②	①	②	③	Ⓐ	③	②	①	②	③
Count	1	+	2	+	3	+	1	+	2	+	3	+
Right Hand	p	i	m	a	m	i	p	i	m	a	m	i

48

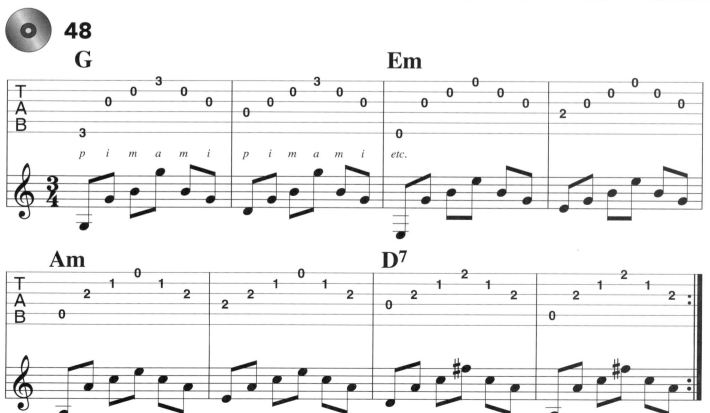

ARPEGGIO PICKING STYLE PATTERNS THREE AND FOUR

The next two arpeggio patterns place another bass note on the third beat. Pattern three repeats the root bass note. Pattern four employs the alternating bass note.

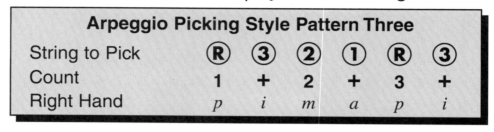

Arpeggio Picking Style Pattern Three						
String to Pick	Ⓡ	③	②	①	Ⓡ	③
Count	1	+	2	+	3	+
Right Hand	p	i	m	a	p	i

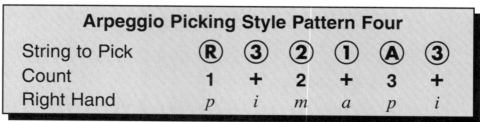

Arpeggio Picking Style Pattern Four						
String to Pick	Ⓡ	③	②	①	Ⓐ	③
Count	1	+	2	+	3	+
Right Hand	p	i	m	a	p	i

Example 49 makes use of the above patterns.

 49

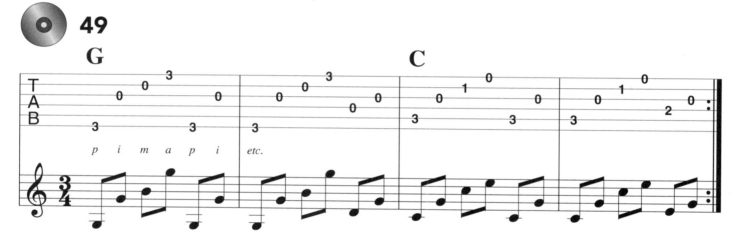

Amazing Grace is another song in ¾ time.

 50 Amazing Grace - Melody

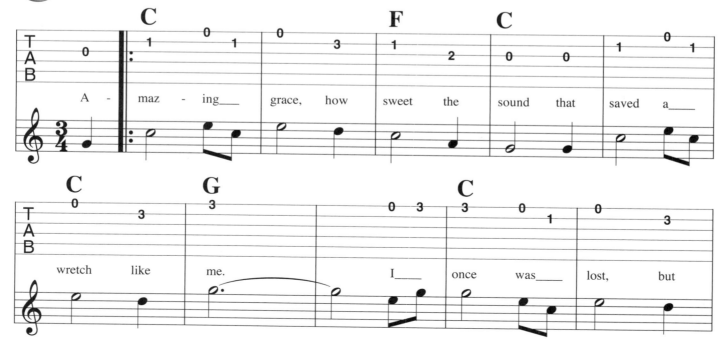

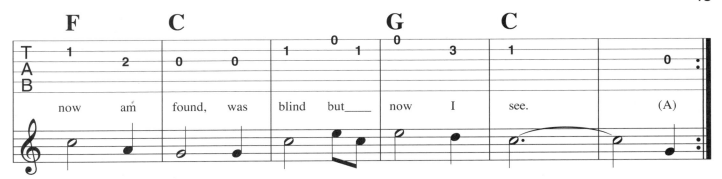

The arpeggio style is used for the accompaniment to *Amazing Grace*.

51 Amazing Grace

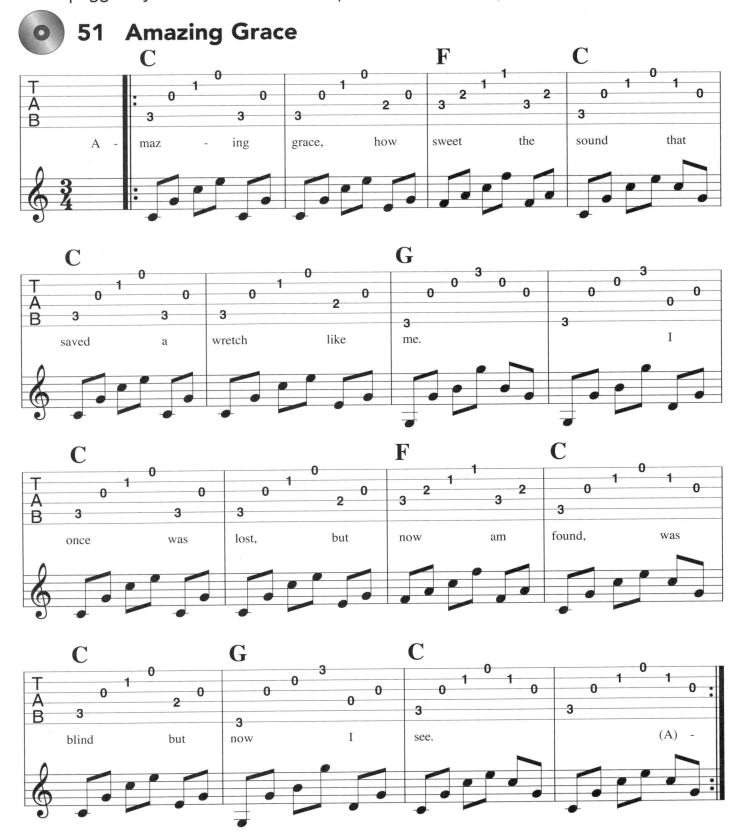

The bass string hammer-on technique introduced on the previous page is featured throughout the following accompaniment.

68 Red River Valley - Accompaniment

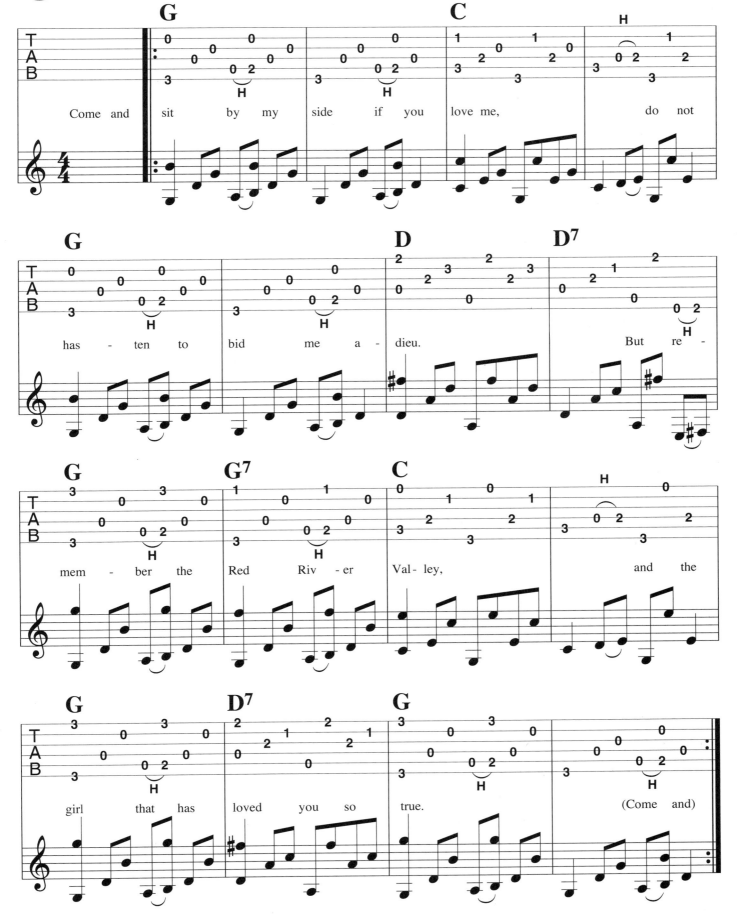

LESSON EIGHT

ADDING EXTRA NOTES TO A CHORD

A fingerpicking pattern can be enhanced by altering the chord shape with the addition of other notes based around the chord. The notes that can be added to a chord shape are normally taken from the respective Major and Blues scales. For information on scales see the back of this book. The term **lick** is used to describe a fingerpicking pattern that incorporates the use of other notes based around the chord.

BASIC G CHORD LICKS

The adjacent diagram highlights the common notes often incorporated into a fingerpicking pattern over a basic G chord. The basic chord shape is only the 3rd finger on the root bass note (6th string) and the fourth finger on the first string. Note that it is not necessary to fret the 5th string bass note (2nd fret). The recommended fingering for the other notes is also shown.

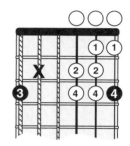

The following example is based upon a basic G chord. Extra notes are incorporated into the fingerpicking pattern to create a G chord lick. Special attention should be given to the suggested left hand fingering.

69

In order to get the correct effect for the following lick do not let the open second string(B) and the note on the third string, 3rd fret(B♭) ring together. Immediately after the B♭ note is sounded lift the fretting finger of the string.

70

BASIC C CHORD LICKS

The adjacent diagram highlights the common notes often incorporated into a fingerpicking pattern over a basic C chord. The basic C chord is fretted as normal with most of the extra notes played with the fourth finger.

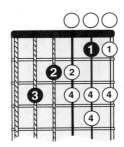

To play the next example hold a basic C chord shape throughout. The other fretted notes in the lick are played with the fourth finger.

  71

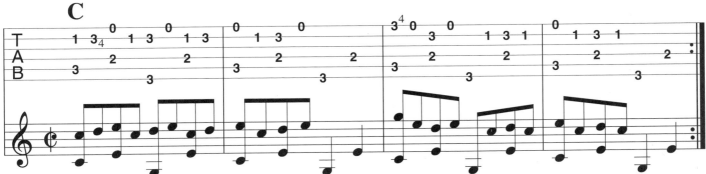

PICKING FOUR NOTES TOGETHER

It is also common practice to pick four strings simultaneously. This is when the right hand fingers pick three treble strings at the same time a bass note is picked. In the adjacent example the *i*, *m* and *a* fingers pick the first three strings at the same time. It is important to pick all strings as evenly as possible so each string has the same volume and tone.

72

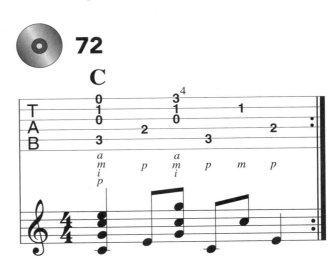

The following C chord lick features the picking of four strings at the same time. A small bass run has also been incorporated in the lick.

73

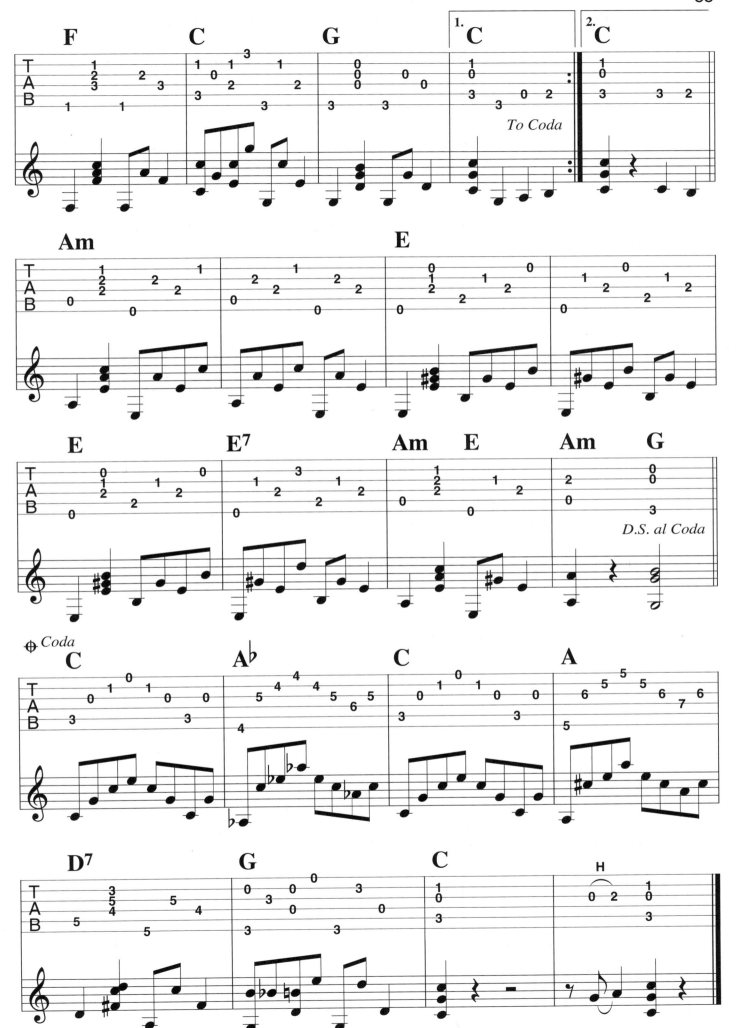

LESSON NINE

FINGERPICKING A MELODY

This lesson will teach you how it is possible to combine a melody line with a bass line and fingerpicking pattern. This technique mostly involves the playing of a melody line on the treble strings. The first example is the popular song *When the Saints Go Marching In*. First practice the melody to this song which is played solely on the first and second strings.

 85 When the Saints Go Marching In - Melody

Now practice bass line that corresponds with the chord progression.

 86 When the Saints Go Marching In - Bass Line

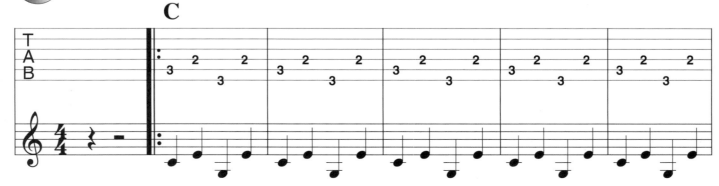

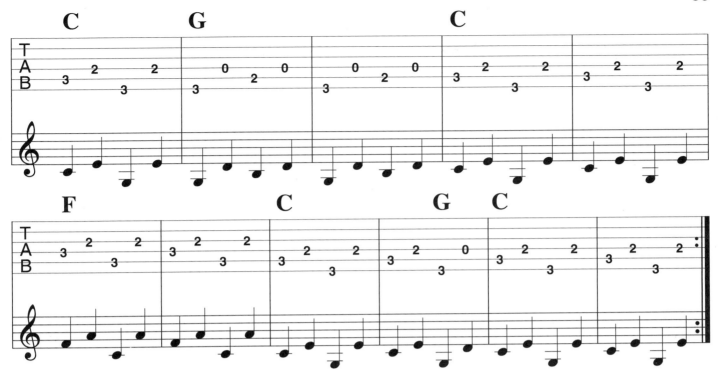

Now try combining the melody and bass line together which requires pinching the melody and bass notes together.

87 When the Saints Go Marching In

The following arrangement of *Oh, Bury Me Not On the Lone Prairie* makes use of the Country bass line pattern introduced in the previous example. This bass line is used in the bars where the melody is played only on the first beat of the bar. Using this bass line is an alternative to playing a basic fingerpicking pattern to fill out the sound. Special attention should be given to the suggested left hand fingering.

7^{CD2} Oh, Bury Me Not On the Lone Prairie

The next song is a traditional American Folk song called *Shenandoah*.

8^{CD2} **Shenandoah - Melody**

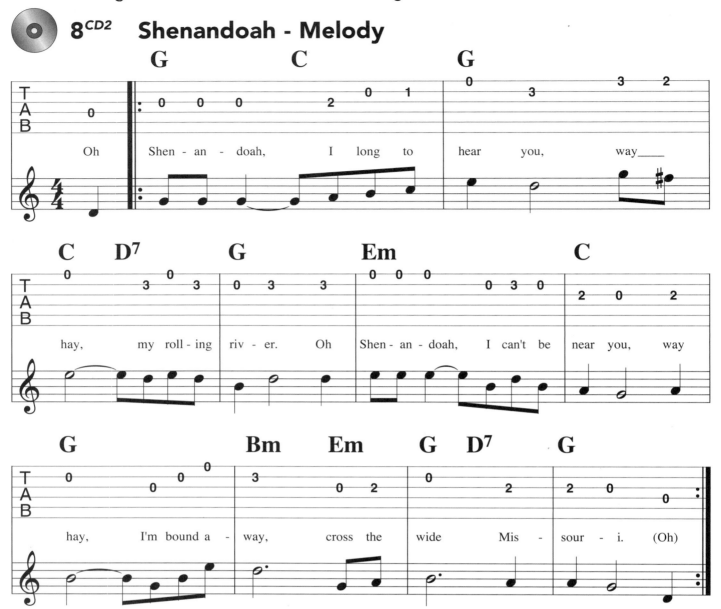

MORE BASS RUNS

There are literally endless ways of using bass runs. One interesting technique is playing two bass notes per beat, sometimes referred to as 'doubling the bass'. This technique is demonstrated in the following example.

9^{CD2}

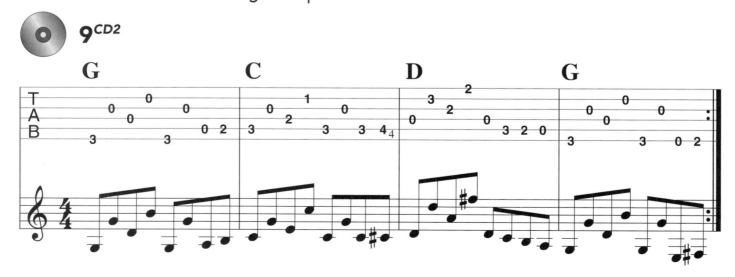

The next arrangement has a bass line that makes use of eighth notes and sixteenth notes.

10^{CD2} Shenandoah

THE TRIPLET RHYTHM

Almost all blues is played to a **triplet rhythm**. This rhythm is created by playing three evenly spaced notes per beat (a total of twelve notes per bar). The first of each three notes is played slightly stronger or louder than the other two notes within a beat. The rhythm is counted **1 and ah 2 and ah 3 and ah 4 and ah**, written as **1 + a, 2 + a, 3 + a, 4 + a**. The triplet rhythm is used in the following lick. Listen carefully to the recording to hear the correct timing and feel for this rhythm.

22^{CD2}

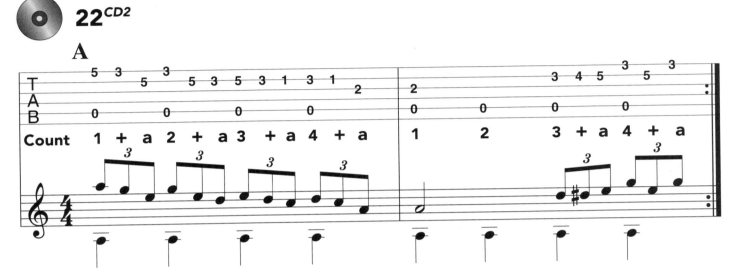

It is also common to miss the middle note within a triplet group. The next example uses a rhythm counted as "**1 ... ah, 2 ... ah, 3 ... ah, 4 ... ah**". Once again, listen carefully to the recording to help with the timing of this rhythm.

23^{CD2}

THE BEND

The **bend** is achieved by bending a string with the left hand in the direction of the adjacent strings, causing the note to rise in pitch. This is done with the left hand finger which is fretting the note. In example 24, the note on the third fret of the 2nd string is bent with the third finger of the left hand. In order to bend the note successfully, bend the string with the help of the second finger as well. The symbol **B** and a curved line indicate a bend. The bracketed fret number indicates the correct pitch the note is to bent.

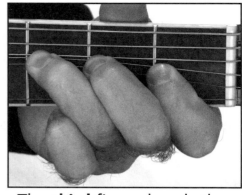

The **third** finger bends the string upwards, with the help of the **second** finger.

24^{CD2}

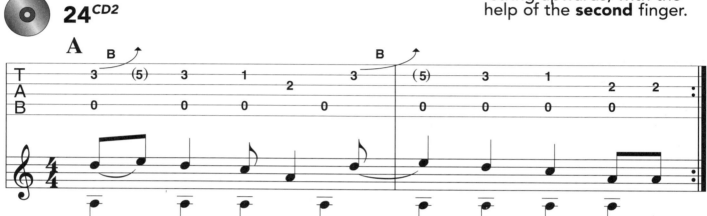

THE RELEASE BEND

The **release bend** is played by first bending the note indicated with the left hand, plucking the string whilst bent, then returning the string to its normal position. If played correctly the release bend creates a drop in pitch from a higher note to a lower note.

A release bend is used in example 25. Bend the note on the 2nd string, third fret with the third finger of the left hand. Pick the 2nd string with the right hand while the string is bent. Immediately after striking the string and still maintaining pressure on the note against the fretboard release the string carefully to its normal position. The release bend is indicated by a curved line and the symbol **R**.

Note: for music readers, when two eighth notes are notated together, the notes are played as the 1st and 3rd parts of a triplet, indicated by the symbol ♪♪ = ♩♪ above the music. This rhythm will apply to almost all the examples, licks and solos that follow in this book.

25^{CD2}

Now a complete 12 bar Blues progression using a variety of techniques.

ADDITIONAL NOTES

The adjacent diagram highlights some additional notes which are often used within the Minor Pentatonic and Blues patterns, position 5. These notes are taken from the Major scale. For more information on scales and patterns see *Progressive Blues Lead Guitar Method*.

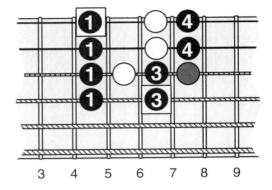

The next example makes use of the additional notes.

41^{CD2}

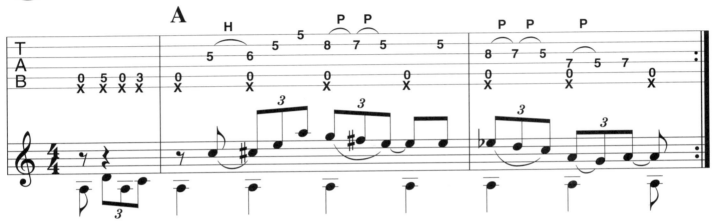

SEVENTH POSITION - KEY OF A

Another useful pattern for the key of A is located between the 7th and 11th frets. The adjacent diagram highlights the Minor Pentatonic pattern. The extra note to complete the Blues scale has also been included in the diagram, along with some additional notes.

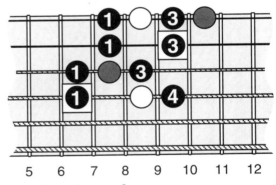

The following example is played within the seventh position, key of A.

42^{CD2}

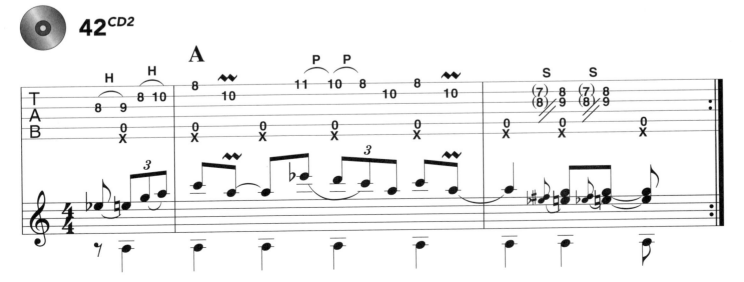

THE COMPLETE PATTERN - KEY OF A

It is now possible to review all three positions introduced in this book for the Minor Pentatonic and Blues scales. The adjacent diagram highlights the Minor Pentatonic notes (black), the extra note to complete the Blues scale (shaded) and the common additional notes found within the patterns.

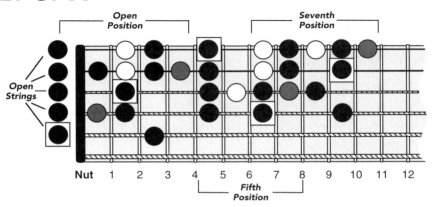

Example 43 shows how the complete pattern, as shown above, can be used to produce a simple, yet great sounding fingerpicking Blues lick. Bass line techniques are also featured.

43^{CD2}

MORE SCALE PATTERNS - KEY OF E

It will also be useful to become familiar with the extended scale patterns in the key of E. The two common extended scale patterns in the key of E are based around the fourth position (frets 4 - 8) and the seventh position (frets 7 - 11).

The Minor Pentatonic scale is highlighted below with the extra note to form the Blues scale highlighted as a shaded dot. The plain dots are additional notes.

FOURTH POSITION - KEY OF E

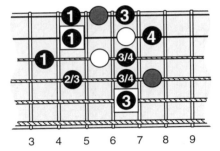

3 4 5 6 7 8 9

SEVENTH POSITION - KEY OF E

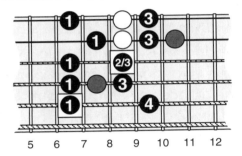

5 6 7 8 9 10 11 12

 44^{CD2}   The next example uses both of the above patterns.

THE COMPLETE PATTERN - KEY OF E

The adjacent diagram highlights the three scale positions so far studied in the key of E.

Ensure you become familiar with this complete pattern and try to create some fingerpicking licks of your own using this pattern.

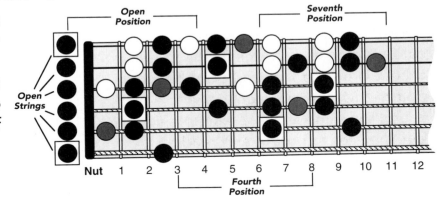

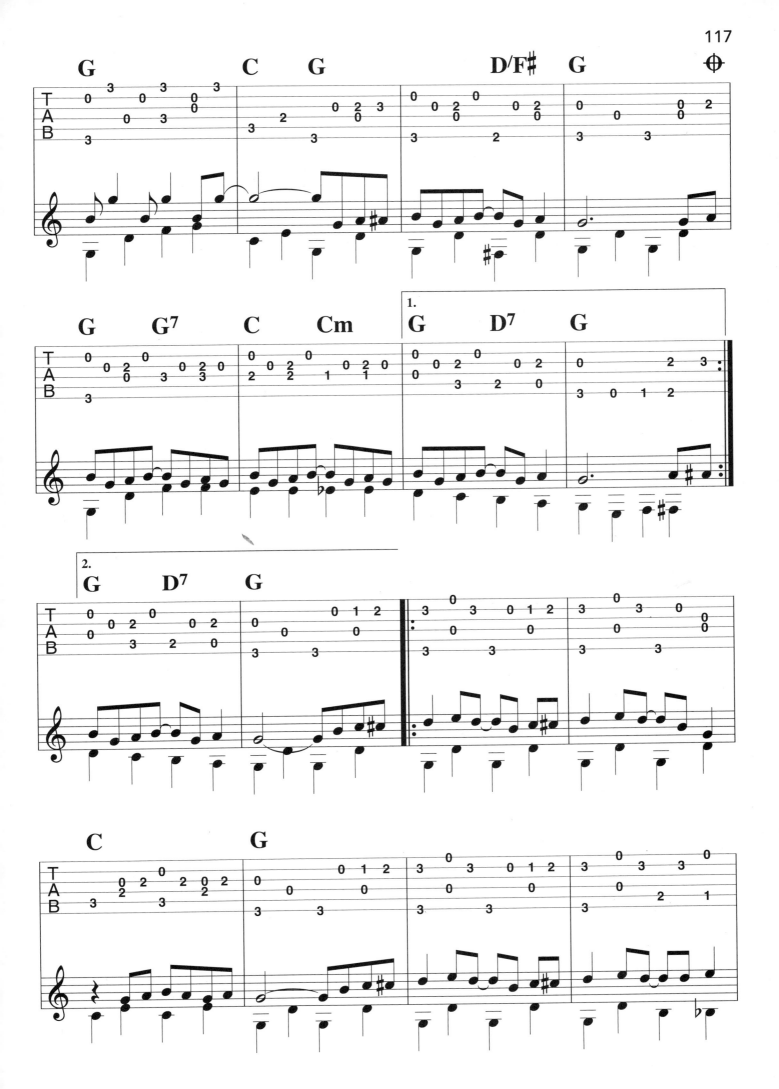

OCTAVES

Another interesting fingerpicking technique is the use of octaves. An octave is the interval between two notes of the same name, 12 frets apart. The adjacent diagram highlights the location of four separate octaves. The four bar introduction to the next arrangement, *Weeping Willow* is played using octaves. Practice the treble and bass parts separately at first before trying to play both parts together.

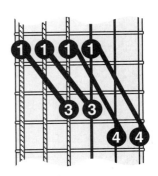

Weeping Willow is another classic rag in the key of G. The first section uses a chord progression similar to the first section of *The Entertainer*. The second section uses chord shapes all over the fretboard and requires some fretting with the left hand thumb. Remember to try the suggested left hand fingering notated in the tab.

58^{CD2} Weeping Willow

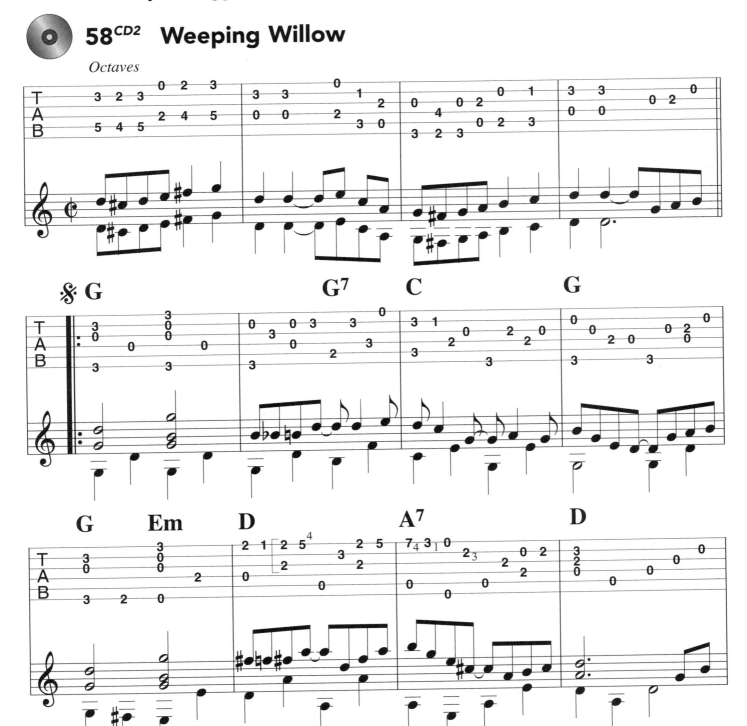

MINOR SEVENTH CHORDS

The next set of chords to learn are the **minor seventh** Jazz chord shapes. Study the adjacent diagrams that highlight the root six and root five minor seventh chords.

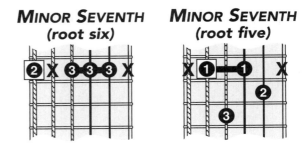

Minor seventh chords feature in the following example. Damping is also recommended on some of the chords. These damping indicators are only suggestions. As you become comfortable with the example you may find you are using alternative damps.

66^{CD2}

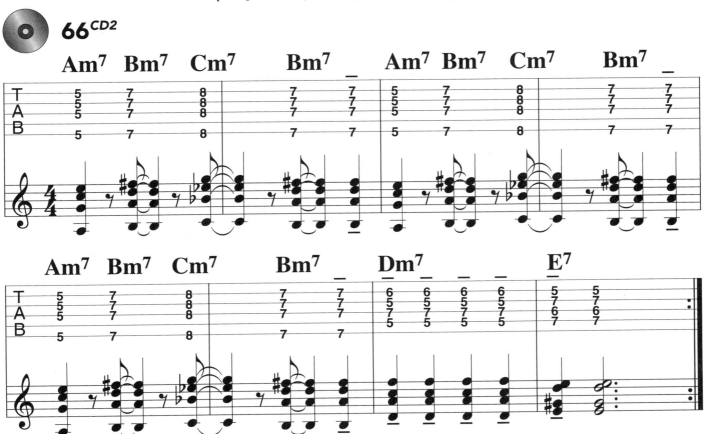

BASS CHORD RHYTHMS

There are a variety of interesting rhythms than can be created using the bass chord style. An example of a **bass chord rhythm** is shown next. Listen carefully to the CD to get the correct timing of this example and try to imitate the damping technique.

67^{CD2}

130

The next progression features another example of a bass chord rhythm.

68.0^{CD2}

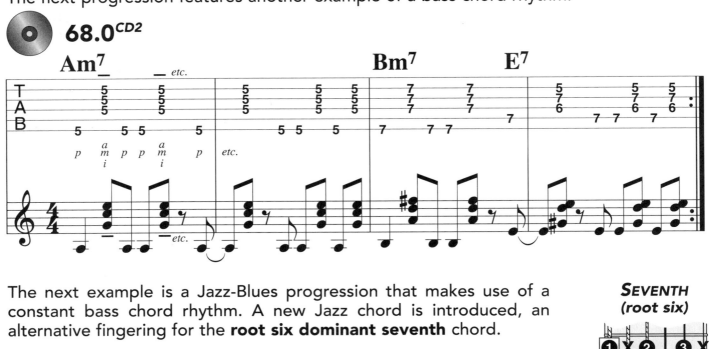

The next example is a Jazz-Blues progression that makes use of a constant bass chord rhythm. A new Jazz chord is introduced, an alternative fingering for the **root six dominant seventh** chord.

SEVENTH (root six)

68.1^{CD2}

MAJOR SEVENTH CHORDS

The next set of chords to learn are the **major seventh** Jazz chord shapes. Study the adjacent diagrams that highlight the root six and root five major seventh chords.

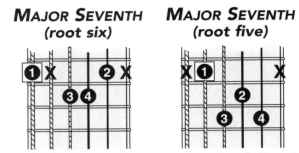

Major seventh chords and a variety of bass chord rhythms feature in the following example. Listen carefully to the CD to get the correct timing of this example and try to imitate the damping technique.

69 CD2

MINOR SEVEN FLAT FIVE

The common Jazz chord shapes for the **minor seven flat five** chord contain the root note on the 6th and 5th strings.

MINOR NINTH

The common Jazz chord shapes for the **seven sharp five** chord contain the root note on the 6th and 5th strings.

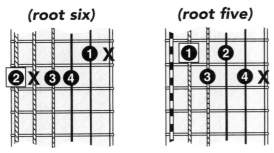

(root six)   (root five)

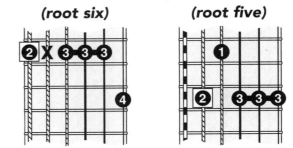

(root six)   (root five)

ALTERNATIVE BASS NOTES

Sometimes a chord can be played using an **alternative bass note** for the root of the chord. The adjacent diagrams highlight two examples of this. The first chord, written as Cmaj7/G is a C major seventh chord with a G bass note. The second chord, D7/A is a D seventh chord with an A bass note.

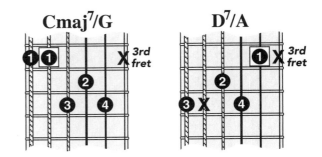

The next example uses a variety of Jazz chords including minor ninth, seventh, seven flat five, major seventh, minor seven flat five and seven sharp five chords. The two alternative bass note chord shapes shown above are also used. You may prefer to use finger rolls for most of the following chord shapes.

82.1^{CD2}

SEVEN SHARP NINE

The common Jazz chord shapes for the **seven sharp nine** chord contain the root note on the 6th and 5th strings.

THIRTEEN FLAT NINE

The common Jazz chord shapes for the **thirteen flat nine** chord do not contain the root note. The diagrams below highlight the closest key note as a reference point.

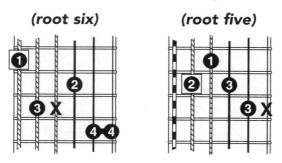

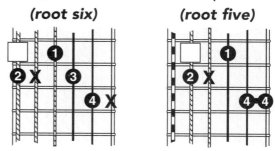

Some of the above chord shapes are used in the following example.

83.0^{CD2}

SEVEN SHARP FIVE FLAT NINE

The common Jazz chord shapes for the **seven sharp five flat nine** chord contain the root note on the 6th and 5th strings.

(root six)   *(root five)*

MAJOR SIX ADD NINE

The common Jazz chord shapes for the **major six add nine** chord contain the root note on the 6th and 5th strings.

(root six)   *(root five)*

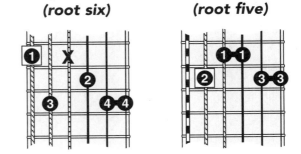

AUGMENTED CHORDS

Augmented chord shapes are similar to diminished chords in the same way that each note in the chord can be the root note, therefore each chord shape has three names. For example, if the first chord on the left is played on the 1st fret, the chord can be named either Gaug (G+), Aaug (A+), or C#aug (C#+). Like diminished chords it is good to use augmented chords based upon one of the adjacent root positions.

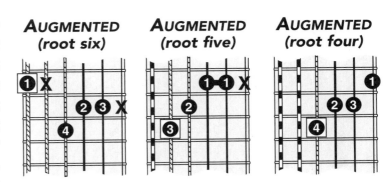

AUGMENTED *(root six)*   **AUGMENTED** *(root five)*   **AUGMENTED** *(root four)*

All of the above chord shape types are used in example 83.1.

83.1 CD2

The final arrangement of *Aura Lee* plays a chord on almost every melody note. The name of the chord changes to suit the melody note. Other techniques such as bass runs and single note runs are also incorporated into the arrangement.

90^{CD2} **Aura Lee - Final Arrangement**

Now try the melody to an old Jazz-Blues classic, *St. James Infirmary.*

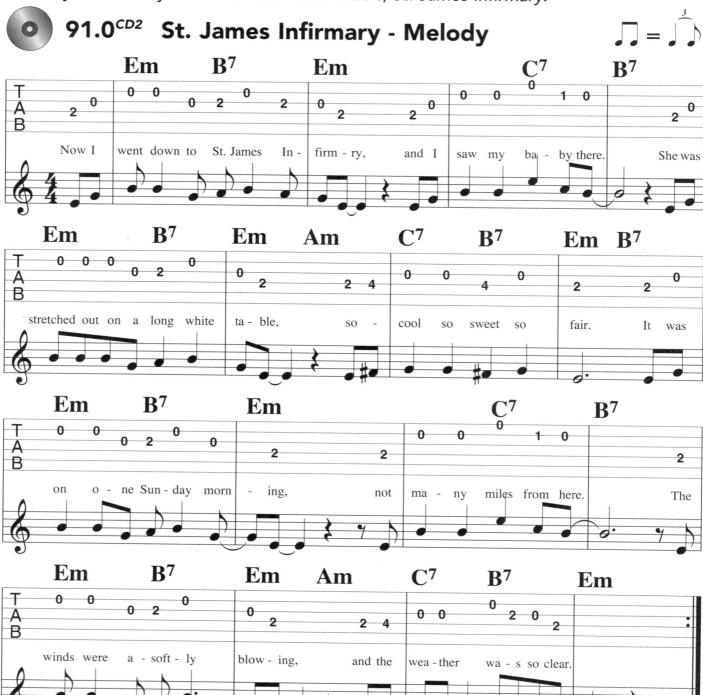

The following Jazz arrangement features the thumb persussion technique.

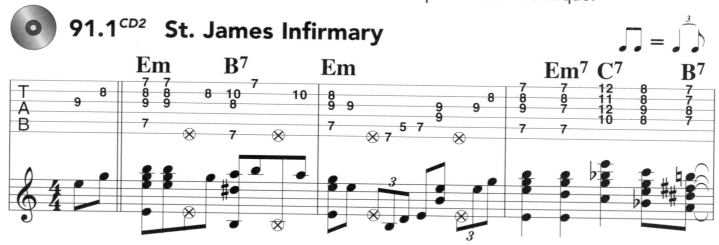

BAR CHORDS - OPEN G TUNING

The most commonly used bar chords in open tuning are based upon the major chord, played simply as a 1st finger bar across all the strings. Various extended chords can be created by adding other fretted notes to the chord shape. Some of the more popular chords are shown below. The key note for open G bar chords is on the fifth string.

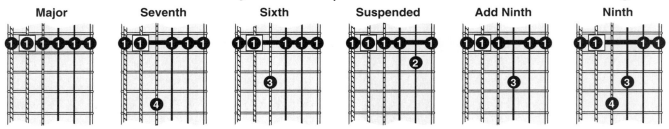

Example 95 makes use of some of the above chord shapes. This is an 8 bar Blues progression based around the open G chord, C on the 5th fret and D on the 7th fret.

The Spanish Spinster is a solo in open G tuning. This piece combines a melody line, an arpeggio picking pattern and a syncopated bass line.

96^{CD2} **The Spanish Spinster**   Tuning - D G D G B D

APPENDICES

SCALES

A scale can be defined as a series of notes, in alphabetical order, going from any given note to its octave and based upon some form of set pattern. The pattern upon which most scales are based involves a set sequence of **tones** and/or **semitones**. On the guitar, a tone is two frets and a semitone is one fret. As an example, the **B** note is a tone higher than **A**, (two frets), whereas the **C** note is only a semitone higher than **B** (one fret). Of the other natural notes in music, **E** and **F** are a semitone apart, and all the others are a tone apart.

NATURAL NOTES

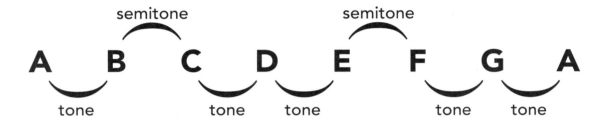

In music theory, a tone may be referred to as a **step** and a semitone as a **half-step**.

The main types of scales that you need to become familiar with are the **chromatic**, **major**, **minor**, **minor pentatonic** and **blues** scales.

THE CHROMATIC SCALE

The **chromatic** scale is based upon a sequence of **semitones** only and this includes every possible note within one octave. Here is the **C chromatic scale**.

C C♯ D D♯ E F F♯ G G♯ A A♯ B C

The same scale could be written out using flats, however it is more common to do this when descending, as such;

C B B♭ A A♭ G G♭ F E E♭ D D♭ C

Because each chromatic scale contains every possible note within one octave, once you have learnt one you have basically learnt them all. As an example, the **A** chromatic scale (written below) contains exactly the same notes as the **C** chromatic scale, the only difference between them being the note upon which they commence. This starting note, in all scales, is referred to as the **tonic** or **key note**.

THE A CHROMATIC SCALE

A A♯ B C C♯ D D♯ E F F♯ G G♯ A

THE MAJOR SCALE

The most common scale in Western music is called the **major scale**. This scale is based upon a sequence of both tones and semitones, and is sometimes referred to as a **diatonic** scale. Here is the major scale sequence;

TONE	TONE	SEMITONE	TONE	TONE	TONE	SEMITONE
T	T	S	T	T	T	S

Starting on the **C** note and following through this sequence gives the **C major** scale;

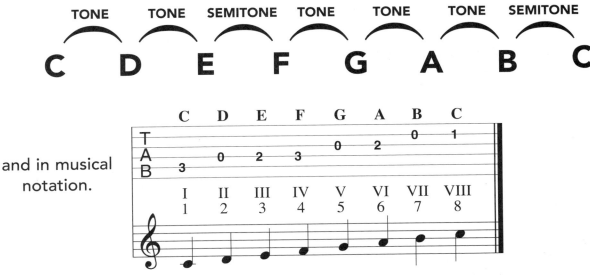

and in musical notation.

Roman numerals are used to number each note of the major scale. Thus **F** is the **fourth** note of the **C major** scale, **G** is the **fifth**, and so on.
The major scale will always give the familiar sound of **DO, RE, MI, FA, SO, LA, TI, DO**.

The major scale **always** uses the same sequence of tones and semitones, no matter what note is used as the tonic. The table below list the 13 most commonly used major scales.

You will notice that, in order to maintain the correct sequence of tones and semitones, all major scales except **C major** involve the use of either sharps or flats. You will notice, when playing these scales, that they all maintain the familiar sound of **DO, RE, MI, FA SO, LA, TI, DO**.

	T	T	S	T	T	T	S
C MAJOR	C	D	E	F	G	A	B	C
G MAJOR	G	A	B	C	D	E	F♯	G
D MAJOR	D	E	F♯	G	A	B	C♯	D
A MAJOR	A	B	C♯	D	E	F♯	G♯	A
E MAJOR	E	F♯	G♯	A	B	C♯	D♯	E
B MAJOR	B	C♯	D♯	E	F♯	G♯	A♯	B
F♯ MAJOR	F♯	G♯	A♯	B	C♯	D♯	E♯	F♯
F MAJOR	F	G	A	B♭	C	D	E	F
B♭ MAJOR	B♭	C	D	E♭	F	G	A	B♭
E♭ MAJOR	E♭	F	G	A♭	B♭	C	D	E♭
A♭ MAJOR	A♭	B♭	C	D♭	E♭	F	G	A♭
D♭ MAJOR	D♭	E♭	F	G♭	A♭	B♭	C	D♭
G♭ MAJOR	G♭	A♭	B♭	C♭	D♭	E♭	F	G♭
Roman Numerals	I	II	III	IV	V	VI	VII	VIII

Mode — a displaced scale e.g. playing through the C to C scale, but starting and finishing on the D note.

Moderato — at a moderate pace.

Modulation — to change the key within a piece.

Natural — a sign (♮) used to cancel out the effect of a sharp or flat. The word is also used to describe the notes **A**, **B**, **C**, **D**, **E**, **F** and **G**; e.g. 'the natural notes'.

Notation — the written representation of music, by means of symbols (music on a staff), letters (as in chord and note names) and diagrams (as in chord illustrations.)

Note — a single sound with a given pitch and duration.

Octave — the distance between any given note with a set frequency, and another note with exactly double that frequency. Both notes will have the same letter name;

Open chord — a chord that contains at least one open string.

'p' — primary finger (thumb). As used for identifying the right hand fingers.

Passing note — connects two melody notes which are third or less apart. A passing note usually occurs on an unaccented beat of the bar.

Phrase — a small group of notes forming a recognizable unit within a melody.

Pitch — the sound produced by a note, determined by the frequency of the string vibrations. The pitch relates to a note being referred to as 'high' or 'low'.

Pivot finger — a finger which remains in position while the other fingers move, when changing chords.

Position — a term used to describe the location of the left hand on the fret board. The left hand position is determined by the fret location of the first finger, e.g. The 1st position refers to the 1st to 4th frets. The 3rd position refers to the 3rd to 6th frets and so on.

Quarter note — a note with the value of one beat in ¼ time, indicated thus ♩ (also called a crotchet). The quarter note rest, indicating one beat of silence, is written: 𝄽 .

Repeat signs — in music, used to indicate a repeat of a section of music, by means of two dots placed before a double bar line:

Rest — the notation of an absence of sound in music.

Rest stroke — where the finger, after plucking the string, comes to rest on the next string (for accenting the note).

Rhythm — the aspect of music concerned with tempo, duration and accents of notes. Tempo indicates the speed of a piece (fast or slow); duration indicates the time value of each note (quarter note, eighth note, sixteenth note, etc.); and accents indicate which beat is more predominant.

Rondo — see form.

Root note — the note after which a chord or scale is named (also called 'key note').

Semitone — the smallest interval used in conventional music. On guitar, it is a distance of one fret.

Sharp — a sign (♯) used to raise the pitch of a note by one semitone.

Simple time — occurs when the beat falls on an undotted note, which is thus divisible by two.

Sixteenth note — a note with the value of quarter a beat in ¼ time, indicated thus ♬ (also called a semiquaver). The sixteenth note rest, indicating quarter of a beat of silence, is written: 𝄿

Slur — sounding a note by using only the left hand fingers.

Staccato — to play short and detached. Indicated by a dot placed above the note:

Staff — five parallel lines together with four spaces, upon which music is written.

Syncopation — the placing of an accent on a normally unaccented beat. e.g.:

Tablature — a system of writing music which represents the position of the player's fingers (not the pitch of the notes, but their position on the guitar). A chord diagram is a type of tablature. Notes can also be written using tablature thus:

| Music Notation | Tablature | Each line represents a string, and each number represents a fret. |

Tempo — the speed of a piece.

Ternary — see form.

Tie — a curved line joining two or more notes of the same pitch, where the second note(s) is not played, but its time value is added to that of the first note.

(1) **(2)**

In Example 2, the first note is held for seven counts.

Timbre — a quality which distinguishes a note produced on one instrument from the same note produced on any other instrument (also called 'tone colour'). A given note on the guitar will sound different (and therefore distinguishable) from the same pitched note on piano, violin, flute etc. There is usually also a difference in timbre from one guitar to another.

Time signature — a sign at the beginning of a piece which indicates, by means of figures, the number of beats per bar (top figure), and the type of note receiving one beat (bottom figure).

Tone — a distance of two frets; i.e. the equivalent of two semitones.

Transcription — to arrange from one instrument to another, i.e. piano - guitar

Transposition — the process of changing music from one key to another.

Treble — the upper regions of pitch in general.

Treble clef — a sign placed at the beginning of the staff to fix the pitch of the notes placed on it. The treble clef (also called 'G clef') is placed so that the second line indicates as G note:

← **G line**

Tremolo — a rapid repetition on one note.

Triplet — a group of three notes played in the same time as two notes of the same kind. e.g.:

Eighth note triplet

count: **1 + a**   **1 +**

Vibrato — a rapid vibration of a note (by the left hand fingers) to create slight pitch variations and a 'wavering' effect.

Whole note — a note with the value of four beats in $\frac{4}{4}$ time, indicated thus ○ (also called a 'semibreve'). The whole note rest, indicating four beats of silence is written: ▬ ← 4th staff line.